# The Message of a Master

**John McDonald**

**John McDonald**

**Filiquarian Publishing, LLC**

# Contents

To the Reader     5

Chapter One     7

Chapter Two     11

Chapter Three     15

Chapter Four     19

Chapter Five     23

Chapter Six     27

Chapter Seven     31

Chapter Eight     35

Chapter Nine     39

Chapter Ten     41

Chapter Eleven                    45

Chapter Twelve                    49

Chapter Thirteen                  53

Chapter Fourteen                  57

Chapter Fifteen                   63

# To The Reader

The following pages are the result of a series of notes collected and set down in the form of a story and a system of practice, which accounts for the style of arrangement. The sequential order as originally received has been carefully adhered to that its value to the reader might not be lessened.

It sets forth no creed or dogma, but teaches in a clear, understandable, simple way, step by step, a practical, workable procedure based upon Divine Law, for the mastery of environment and conditions.

Surely, there is an unexplainable "something" within its pages which carries a wonderful power for helpfulness and which saturates the reader with a dynamic realization and conviction of what it teaches.

This is not a volume to be hurriedly or superficially read. It must be studied in order to gain the priceless wisdom which it contains. Therefore it is strongly urged that, after having been read through once or twice, it be given the slow, deep, deliberate study which has proved to be the profitable way with a work of this kind.

Read it as though it were a message directed to none but yourself. Try to reason out each proposition to your own satisfaction and to get the spirit back of the words. Then apply its teachings to fit your own individual nature and understanding.

During your perusal of these pages should any ideas occur to you concerning your work or ambitions, it is well to lay the book aside for a few moments and meditate upon them. Many profitable ideas have come to readers in this way.

# Chapter One

Presuming that there are many who are just as skeptical concerning things bordering on the extraordinary as I have been practically all of my life, I offer the following story and system of practice to each reader for what it is worth, with the suggestion that he take it or leave it, just as he sees fit.

It was Saturday afternoon and I had returned from a late lunch. The help had left for the day and I was alone. My business had dropped off considerably of late and while conditions were not alarming, yet they were sufficient to cause me some concern. Then again, I had recently indulged in some real estate speculation which had not proved successful. Taking it all in all, it was not a very cheerful outlook. In fact the most serious problem of my business career was up for solution.

Sitting there in deep thought in an effort to discover a way out, I was aroused by the telephone bell. Placing the receiver to my ear I was startled at hearing the familiar voice of my old friend, David Bentley. It required no great stretch of the imagination to believe it a voice from the dead, for less than a month before he had left for Europe on the urgent advice of his physician to take an ocean voyage, preferably, but get away somewhere, in the hope that a change would effect an improvement in his condition, which was a serious breakdown, due to worry over conditions which, strangely, were similar to what I was now experiencing.

As he spoke, his voice carried such striking power and feeling that I was reminded of my last impression of Dave as we sorrowfully parted with him, a miserable shadow of his former self, and we questioned as to whether we would ever see him again.

But here he was back again, and surely some great change had taken place in him. Remarking that a miracle must have happened, he assured me that I had guessed about right, adding, "Tom, I know that you are puzzled over my early return and I also know that you never expected to see me again. But I'm back and I'm the luckiest man in the world, for I learned something that I never knew existed. "Tom, nothing is impossible with me any more, for I can do anything. I am master of my own destiny and I can make my life anything that I wish it to be.

"Oh, don't think I'm crazy. Wait until you hear my story." Feigning a laugh to cover my serious curiosity, I remarked that he must have stumbled over some newfangled religion. To which he replied, "On the contrary, it concerns no religion of any kind or of anybody. You see, I met a Master. A wonderful man who has so developed his powers that he can do anything, and he taught me a secret that no price could ever buy. You know that I lost my health and I lost my wealth. Well, I have regained my health and I will have the wealth in no time. Oh, it's a strange story." Of course I became excited to see him at

**8**

once and when to his inquiry about the club I replied that there were no changes, he hung up after saying, "Meet me there at 9:00 tonight and I will unfold a series of the most remarkable and fortunate happenings that could fall to the lot of any man."

I sat there unmoved for some minutes like a man in a dream, so completely absorbed had I become in the remarkable recital. Upon recovering myself I became possessed of the feeling that I had suddenly grown too big for the office. That I had outgrown that little place. I must get outside and expand in the fresh air. Feverish with excitement, I put on my hat and stepped out. Feeling that there was something wonderful for me in his story, I was seized with an uncontrollable desire to hear it at once. I turned in the direction of his office, but recalling that he was no longer there, was forced to wait until evening. The remainder of that day was spent in restlessly pacing the streets and I was greatly relieved when the hour to go to the club arrived.

Having resolved to get Dave away where we would not be disturbed, I entered and stepped quickly to the desk, only to be informed that he had telephoned some time before to tell me that he had been called away and would be back the following evening. Trying to conceal my feelings of disappointment, I turned quickly and was greeted by three friends who had seen him, and each was excitely trying to tell me of the wonders that had taken place. Miserable and disconsolate, I broke away from them without uttering a word, walked out into the night and home.

Too agitated for sleep, the greater part of the night was passed in restless confusion. Assailed by the most illogical thoughts, I decided that the whole thing was a myth, conjured up in a mind weakened as the result of affliction. How utterly ridiculous to allow myself to become upset by such a fairy tale. But no, somehow the thing would not go away, but kept forcing itself upon me, until in desperation I tried to console myself with the assurance that I would at any cost learn the truth or falsity of the whole matter the next day.

# Chapter Two

Following instructions which I had left at the club to be delivered to him immediately upon his return, Dave picked me up at my home in a new, high-priced car, and we drove out to a high way cafe. There, in a private dining room, undisturbed by the presence of others, I had opportunity to study my old friend.

Surely some miraculous change had taken place in him. His countenance allowed with health and vitality and his calm, poised bearing inspired wonderful admiration and confidence. But while I felt perfectly at ease in his company, I also felt the force of some presence in him that I could neither understand nor describe. Whatever it was, it had the effect of putting one at ease and yet had the tendency to command respect for something one did not understand. While I felt greatly relieved after the excitement of the previous day, yet I found difficulty in concealing the emotions that surged up within me, for I felt satisfied and convinced that he had something that I sorely needed and I had the strangest fear lest something might occur even then to prevent my getting it.

He broke a momentary silence that seemed hours to me by asking, "Tom, do I look any different than the day I left?" I had to admit that he was both a revelation and a mystery to me. He continued, "It was in a theatre in London that I met the man, or the Master, as he is called, that I am deeply grateful for the privilege of calling my friend. Tom, you didn't know that I left here determined to end it all. I had made such a mess of my affairs. But I feared to live and I feared to die. I couldn't rest. To keep moving was my only relief. I guess I was what the world would call a hopeless case.

"As I look back upon that evening in London, how well I now realize that my utter despondency and the intense longing to find something to relieve me drew me and my dear friend together. I had decided upon a regular orchestra seat, but discovered that for some unexplainable reason I had ordered a box and found myself seated beside my friend. Extraordinary happenings, such as this, occur frequently to many of us and are explained away, because of our ignorance, as merely coincidences. But I know differently now.

"I could feel that my uneasiness attracted his attention. The wonderful radiance of his countenance assured that he was an unusual personage and I felt an instinctive urge to open my heart to him. The remark, 'I am sorely troubled,' uttered by a character upon the stage started our acquaintance. I replied 'so am I,' in just a whisper, but my friend heard it and turning to me he asked, 'are you troubled?' I nodded my head in response and you may believe me or not, but almost immediately I was at ease. Something seemed to tell me that I had the good fortune of being in the presence of one of those great spiritual people of whom I had read quite a bit in earlier years.

"I felt convinced that I had met my deliverer, and at the close of the performance was overjoyed at his invitation to accompany him to a nearby café. I noticed that the attention of those in the café was drawn toward him as we entered and that the management was noticeably respectful and courteous toward him. Having convinced myself that this man possessed some sort of magical power, I determined to ask him all the questions that I could think of and with his permission make notes of his answers.

"Learning that he was taking a steamer for New York the next day, I asked if I might accompany him, to which he assented. At the conclusion of our talk I observed that he merely wrote his initials on the bill and as we stepped outside to call a cab I questioned him regarding this and he admitted that he was not known there, as this was his first visit to the place, but he assured me that they would be paid, adding, 'I did this to show you that man in his right domain controls every situation.' I was still puzzled, but carried the subject no further, hoping that it would all be made plain to me later.

"That night, as I lay in a doze, the events of the evening kept passing through my mind and at times I found it difficult in realizing that my good fortune was real, rather than the illusion of a dream. That night I had the first peaceful sleep in months."

**John McDonald**

# Chapter Three

The following morning, up early and supremely happy and eager for what the day would unfold, I immediately applied for a reservation on the steamer, only to be informed that they had a full passenger list, but as I turned away, almost heartbroken at such an unfortunate turn of events, I was recalled by the clerk with the information that a reservation had just been cancelled and that I might have it. Instantly I felt forcibly struck with the thought that here was more of my friend's 'magic,' as I then called it, and I was not mistaken, for he later admitted that he had made a place for me. Of course, you do not understand how the thing works, Tom. Neither did I, at the time, but I do now, and it is oh, so simple. I believe its simplicity causes it to be overlooked.

"Presently my friend arrived, with servant, and, as usual, being surrounded by attendants eager to be of service and assistance. I clung to him persistently throughout the entire voyage, and he appeared to enjoy my company.

"The first evening out, I visited him in his luxuriously-furnished stateroom, for he has the best of everything wherever he goes, and while explaining the wonderful forces that man in his ignorance has permitted to lie dormant within him, he gave me several demonstrations of the powers that he has developed. He did things that were actually astounding. He asked, 'Why cannot you do what I do? Why cannot all do as I do? I have no powers that you are not endowed with. Here is my answer. Because of my knowledge of Universal Law, I have developed the God-given powers within me, while you, in your ignorance, have been dissipating and scattering yours. All men use the same power, for in all the universe there is but one power. This is self-evident, as you shall see.'

"Continuing, he said: 'the great masses of humanity are using the Law destructively, or partially so, and the scales are balanced against them. Here and there, among the masses, we find an occasional outstanding figure who has achieved greatness or success and he is erroneously singled out as lucky or as a genius, when the fact is that he has made use of the Law – whether knowingly or unknowingly, it matters not – at least sufficiently to have the scales balanced in his favor. How plain this is to the one who knows.'

"Before the discovery of the law governing the use of electricity this great force was lying dormant throughout the universe, at least as far as man's knowledge was concerned. He had first to discover the law before he could turn it to his advantage. Just so with this Universal Law.

" 'Happiness is man's rightful heritage. It is the summum bonum of his aspirations. The very soul of man cries out for happiness, but he misinterprets it in terms of money. Why? Because money is a means to an end. It is the motive power which drives us on in our quest for the ultimate, which is happiness. In the world there cannot be happiness without money. Therefore the occupation of acquiring money is a worthy and commendable one.

"Why should man, the supreme creation of the universe, suffer all sorts of lack, misery and unhappiness when such inferior creatures as the beasts of the field, the birds of the air and the fish of the sea are bountifully supplied. For any man, no matter what his station in life, to take the stand that it is the destiny of man to want for anything that will contribute to his happiness or that of his family is ridiculous.

"Somebody discovers the law governing the use of etheric waves and we have radio. Millions of people are now enjoying its advantages. They tune in to what they want and they get it. There is a great lesson in this, for believe me, you may have anything you want and in abundance, when you learn to tune in with an infinitely greater power than electricity or its vehicle, radio. With a power that you have had from the beginning.

"The captain of this ship could just as easily own it as run it. One position is no more difficult of attainment than the other. He tuned in to the captaincy successfully. Ownership was a little more distant and he did not try for distance. That is all. The actual difference in the two positions is merely the difference in two words. Nothing more, as you shall see very plainly when we get a little further along.'

"Each night, after retiring to my room, I would sit up until early morning reading my notes of the day and preparing questions for the next. He told me that I was very 'receptive' because of my eagerness, sincerity and trust, and that it was a pleasure to instruct me. And in gratitude I acknowledged that no price was too high or sacrifice too great in return for such knowledge.

"In answer to my question as to when and how he discovered such a secret, he said, 'I discovered nothing and to me it is no secret. This knowledge has been in our family as far back as our records go. I use it because I know it to be the easy, certain way of accomplishing a purpose, while you have known only the difficult, uncertain way.' He seemed never to want to take credit for anything, always claiming that no credit was due him.

# Chapter Four

"I was rapidly regaining my health and strength and was becoming fired with an irresistible ambition to get back and start all over again. Censuring myself for having wasted so many valuable years in fruitless effort in my old way, I was eager to start in the new way. Approaching the end of our voyage and feeling that I was soon to part from my great benefactor, to whom I had become greatly attached and to whom I owed so much, I handed him my card and asked for his, to which he replied, 'I have no card, no name, no address. I am like the wind. I come from nowhere and I go everywhere. As for my name, you may call me Friend.' Saying that I would much prefer to call him Master, he replied, 'No, no, not Master. Just Friend. That will do.' Glancing at my card, he said, 'I turn up at the most unexpected places. I might be out to see you soon. If I do, I will write to you.'

"I shall never forget the parting instructions that he gave me. In a manner like a parent with a child, he said, 'You are indeed a fortunate man. Just think of the millions of gifted, highly talented people, many blessed with rare qualities for success and leadership whose achievements would mean so much to their fellow men and happiness and contentment to themselves and their families who do not know what you know. But who go on striving and straining, wasting their precious life force, only to find themselves dissatisfied, discouraged, disheartened, crushed, as you once were, yet spurred on by that divine spark, that irresistible urge within by which they instinctively realize that there is a way but which they, in their ignorance, misinterpret and consequently find themselves failures after years of despairing effort.

"All this you can now avoid. Go home. You have learned all that you will need. If you will diligently follow the instructions that I have given, you may reach any heights. You may accomplish any worthy purpose easily and quickly. There need be no limit to your possibilities. Your successes will multiply and increase in proportion to your master of the Law. With each success your faith in the Law grows stronger until you reach the point of conviction. Then you are invincible.

"Bear in mind the warning that I have repeatedly given you. Reveal nothing of this to even your dearest friend. To do so before you are powerfully fortified in the Law would only tend to interfere with your plans, but particularly, it would result in the scattering of your forces and consequently weaken their power for your good. Therefore, keep your secret securely locked within your heart. You will never be able to work out another's problems. Neither will another be able to work out yours. This is strictly a matter for each individual. Accomplishment of anything, in any line, is the result of the operation of this inner force, discovered and set to work, and this must be done by each one for himself. There is no other way.

"When the time arrives that you shall have retired from commercial pursuits, you may, after seeking the guidance of your conscience, release it for the benefit of others. Thus liberated from further commercial allurements, you will be free to devote your life to the uplift of your fellow man, lending your help to freeing him from the bondage of want, misery and unhappiness.'

"Reluctantly parting with my benefactor as he entered a taxi with his servant and gave directions to this hotel, I started down the street unconscious of the crowds and with such a peculiar sensation of exaltation and buoyancy that I seemed to be just floating along rather than walking. Sleep had no attraction for me and it was with difficulty that I induced myself to retire to a hotel.

"On the train speeding home I carefully avoided all unnecessary contact with my fellow passengers. I kept to my stateroom. Oh, how I wanted to be alone and to think. I could not think of sparing any of my precious time for worthless, idle conversation and gossip. How useless it seemed to me now, when there was so compelling a purpose to try out my new teaching and not another day could be wasted. Nothing else interested me and nothing else mattered.

"There you have as much of my story as I am at liberty to reveal at this time, and I give you this much in the hope that it will encourage you to such an extent that you will consider any personal sacrifice well worth the price of such knowledge. For years I have been blindly seeking what I never imagined existed, and now that I have it, no fortune is large enough to buy it."

**21**

Noticing upon me the appalling effect of his inability to enlighten me further, Dave attempted to ease my feelings with the assurance that he would see that I got in touch with the Master upon his arrival. This only intensified my determination as I excitedly exclaimed, "I'll never wait for an arrival that might never occur. By the gods I'll find him if you will give me the name of his hotel." So different from his former excitable nature, he remained calm and poised as he replied that he had not overheard the name.

# Chapter Five

There was nothing for me to do now but settle down as best I could to impatiently waiting and hoping while he immediately plunged into his former occupation, that of operating in the market. Because of his secretiveness we knew little of his affairs, although we met him a few times at the club. On such occasions, none of us seemed to have the courage to question him regarding himself and he talked on every subject but that. However, it was but a short time until his activities reached such proportions that he was compelled to carry on his operations to some extent through a few of his close friends, including myself. It was then that I learned in part the magnitude of them.

Fearing that such successes could not last, I attempted to advise greater caution, warning him that some day his bubble would burst and then where would he be. With a quick turn toward me, and with his characteristic dominant expression, he replied, "Tom, you need have no concern about my welfare. I operate according to definite unerring law. If you want to get the square feet contained in this room, you would get the two dimensions, and following a process laid down by the law of mathematics, you would arrive at a definite result. You would be certain of the success of the process from the beginning. Just so with my work. I know the outcome before I start." That was the last mention I ever made to him of his affairs and he never referred to them.

There seemed to be no stopping to him, for he went on from one success to another. His perpetual energy and vitality seemed to never lay and the dynamic force with which he seemed to dominate every situation and overwhelm all opposition to his progress was actually superhuman. At the few social gatherings which he attended, his magnetic personality and the mystery with which his name was associated made him the centre of attention.

Because of his desire to avoid notice, I saw little of him for some time and hearing no news of the Master, I had just about become resigned to my fate when one day his secretary telephoned that there was a letter at his office which would interest me. Hurrying over, I was handed a letter, written on the stationery of a prominent hotel and addressed to him, which read: "Detained by important affairs. Regret to have to forego a visit with you this time." And signed, "Your Friend."

At last my chance had come. The hotel was my only clue, but it was enough. Hastily getting my three interested associates together, we left, and that evening found us speeding eastward in our quest of the Master and the "secret." Entering the hotel, upon our arrival, I went direct to the manager and informed him of our mission. He knew immediately and told me that because of the many visitors who were crowding the Master he had departed, leaving no address. He had no further information to give us.

Again I was thoroughly disheartened. Was I ever to learn that "secret?" I really believed that I was not. However, we got a good description of him and decided to continue our search. We separated in order to work more effectively, but our search was without success until the night of the fifth day. I sat alone in the lobby of our hotel that night after my associates had retired, following an hour of argument in an effort to persuade me to return home. I decided that I would not give up. I would continue the search forever, if necessary.

Sitting there in a deserted corner at that hour in the early morning my feelings suddenly changed from utter despondency to joyous elation. Somehow I knew that my search was at an end and while pondering over this I became possessed of a sense of some presence behind me. Immediately, a hand touched my shoulder. I arose, turned, and there before me, I looked into the most magnificent face that I have ever seen. And the eyes! They sparkled like jewels. And a voice said, "Are you looking for me?" I merely answered, "I am," for I knew it was he.

I will not go into his explanation of the causes which led up to our meeting, but after a long talk, during which he explained that his time was so busily occupied that there was no way in which he could give any instructions; that he was not even receiving visitors during this short visit to this country, but that he would advise me of his next visit, I vehemently exclaimed with all the intensity of my being that I was desperately in need of him; that we had come thousands of miles to learn his wisdom and that I was willing to sacrifice anything for just a little of his knowledge. My desperation and the intensity of my appeal must have aroused his compassion, for he agreed to receive us for instructions the following morning at his apartment.

# Chapter Six

The sight that met our eyes as we entered his apartment that morning will stand out vividly in my memory. Never before or since have I seen such luxuriance and extravagance displayed as in the furnishings of that place. It seemed like desecration to tread upon those magnificent silk rugs as we were led by his servant through a room delicately perfumed and an abundance of flowers artistically arranged, to a room which appeared to be his study and where chairs had already been placed for us.

His entry immediately after was followed by a round of introductions, names, occupations and general remarks. We had expected to see him attired in some gorgeous style in keeping with his surroundings, but were struck by the simplicity in both his dress and his bearing. My impression was that being conscious of his power, he preferred to shun publicity and people rather than be the object of any attention and he explained the presence of the furnishings by saying that he loved beautiful things and therefore surrounded himself with them.

He began our instructions by saying, "You may have come here in expectation of seeing a mysterious being endowed with mystic powers. A sort of magician who can pull a fortune out of the air and pass it over to you. You have very much misled yourselves. I am just an ordinary man, no different than you are. The world calls such as me, a Master. And so I am, but only in the sense that I have learned how to master environment and conditions. That I have developed in me the powers that abide alike in all of us and that I am more nearly living life as it should be lived.

"I realize that you have come here because of your faith in me and that you look upon me somewhat as an exalted personality. But in order that you may gain the greatest benefit from these teachings I will ask that you wipe out any impression that you may have of me as a personality. I assure you that I am worthy of no honor or homage. I am just a human like yourself. I am not a superior being. Rather, I am a humble being, thankful for the knowledge that I have gained. I made no discoveries. I received these instructions in much the same manner that I am about to give them to you.

"You will find no difficulty in putting these principles into practice in your everyday affairs. They are as available to you as to me, for this great Law is no respecter of persons. It is the highest and most effective possible in worldly affairs and is well worth learning, for its practice results in a life that is well worth living.

"Employing these principles wisely and intelligently, there can be no uncertainty as to the outcome of any undertaking and no limit to your possibilities. As you go on and on, your confidence increases and you find that your powers are increasing. You accomplish greater things with greater ease and greater speed. As its growth in you increases, your accomplishments increase likewise.

"With many, remarkable improvement comes quickly as in the case of your friend who is responsible for you being here today. With others, the growth is more gradual. The difference is not any difference in the individual, for all are endowed with the same capacity, but it is a difference in the degree of intensity employed. However, no man could ever receive these instructions and not become a better man because of them.

"No greater things are accomplished in the consciousness of personality. That is impossible, for personality is limiting. Therefore, accept these lessons for just what they mean to you alone as an individual entity. Let not my presence of your impression of me influence you in any way in your studies. Learn from my words only, not from me. Now let us proceed.

**John McDonald**

# Chapter Seven

In imparting the principles of this law to you, I will ask that you overlook any apparent contradictions, for, of necessity, they are bound to occur when treating upon a subject of this kind in order that propositions otherwise obscure may be made clear. And again, you must understand that I am using your language to convey my meaning and I meet with some difficulty in doing so. I want you to bear in mind this advice:

Take these teachings for just what they mean to you individually. If some statements do not appear to you at this time, make no effort to force yourself to accept them. What you might reject or fail to understand now will no doubt appear plain and become valuable to you later, as your capacity to receive increases.

There are times when the changing of words makes a subject more clear and appealing to people of different mentalities. Therefore, if you find that the replacing of my words for your own at times makes any statement clearer or seems to fit in with your particular mental make-up or belief, you may do so, freely.

He who is wise in his own conceit, who approaches a subject in an attitude of doubt and resistance, will learn little. There is not much hope for him. But he who takes up any subject in an open mind, willing to learn anything that will contribute to his advancement, comfort and happiness, is wise.

Therefore, while I do not ask that you believe all that I tell you, for to do so would be to intrude upon your God-given freedom of thought, yet neither do I wish you to doubt or resist what I tell you, for that would prevent you from gaining the help you are seeking. For your own highest and greatest good, your attitude should be just this: I am going to take these teachings in an open-minded, neutral attitude, determined that I shall gain all the benefit there is in them for me. The fact that I do not understand or even believe any particular statement or proposition at this time, does not necessarily make it any the less true.

To be able to make use of the Law as outlined, it is necessary that you have a clear understanding of its operation. To this end, I will illustrate, wherever possible, the different propositions with examples in nature that you will find all about you and that will help you in reasoning out these truths to a logical conclusion.

Your mind, which is yourself, can be likened to a house which the accumulation of years has cluttered with thousands of unnecessary pieces of furniture, pictures, ornaments and other things, all strewn around and heaped everywhere, with the result that while the outside of that house might present a good appearance, the inside is a mass of confusion and disorder. How utterly impossible to accomplish anything under such conditions, for you cannot go after one thing without stumbling over another. No order. No purpose. No progress. The first necessary move, then, is to rid that house of all but the furnishings essential to success.

**John McDonald**

# Chapter Eight

How did you get here? You grew from a minute cell smaller than the point of a pin. Just think! A cell or seed the size of a pin point contained within itself in essence and in entirety, the wonderful being that you are today.

Surely, that cell could not possibly contain the material forms, no matter how infinitesimal they might be, of body, head, hair, arms, legs, hands, feet and all the wonderful organs of the body.

Well, then, how did you arrive at your full stature as you now appear? There is but one logical answer – that cell contained a spark of Mind, the one and only power supreme in man. That spark of mind, true to the law of its own being, held a fixed image or picture of you and you unfolded, grew and eventually out-pictured or become objectified in obedience to that law.

Surely, you cannot reasonably deny that, in the process of nature, you originated in a cell. And you will not deny that you could not be contained bodily in that cell. Therefore, the only conclusion is, that you must have been in that cell mentally.

Should your understanding fail to immediately grasp this truth, your reasoning faculty will readily admit that there is a power at work in that cell unfolding according to a definite plan. So intelligence must be present. Admitting the presence of intelligence, it follows that we must admit of the presence of Mind.

It is necessary at this point to get one fact clearly before you, for it is the fundamental basis from which we proceed, and that clearly is this: that Mind, no matter what form it is apparently contained in, holds images, pictures. And any picture firmly held in any mind, in any form, is bound to come forth.

This is the great, unchanging Universal Law which, when we cooperate with it intelligently, makes us absolute masters of conditions and environment.

Can you not recall instances when you have secretly expressed a desire within yourself for some particular thing or that you might meet a particular person, when shortly, that thing becomes your possession or that person appears, and you might exclaim: "Isn't it a coincidence? I was thinking of you just this morning!" It is no coincidence at all. Not at all strange. It was the natural outcome of the operation of definite law.

If this be true, why do not all wishes or thoughts appear? Many do, but because of the absence of alertness, due to ignorance of the law, they pass unnoticed. And again, many do not manifest at all. To illustrate this, I can use your knowledge of radio. You attempt to tune in to one station for some delightful music, but because of there being a number of others on the air, your reward is a jumble of confusion. But should you reach that station when others are temporarily off, you get it clearly and your desire is gratified.

The answer to the question is this: It happened that, by chance, those thoughts or desires which appeared arose at just the instant when there were no other conflicting thoughts present to nullify their power, and the mind, instead of being divided among many thoughts, threw its great force in with the one and it became out-pictured or externalized.

You have experienced times when your mind became a complete blank for just a moment and you found yourself staring out into space. If at that instant it were possible to inject any wish, any desire, with sufficient force, nothing upon earth could prevent it from coming forth instantly.

Now, what is the cause of the confusion prevailing in mind which weakens your thoughts? It is the false belief that there is a power of powers outside of you greater than the power within you. If through a system of practice, conditions within you became such that every constructive thought automatically out-pictured, you would be master of all conditions or circumstances that in any way concerned you or affected your life. Would you not?

**John McDonald**

# Chapter Nine

The next step in your instructions is this: The consciousness or fixed picture in mind of anything, any condition, any circumstance, is the actual thing itself and what you experience through the five senses is the mental picture out-pictured, or made visible or tangible identically the same as the artist who puts his mental pictures upon the canvas; the hand, in his case, being merely the instrument through which the mind expresses and which is under the guidance and direction of the mind.

Does not medical science agree that the human body undergoes a complete change every eleven months? This means that the cells of which your entire body is composed die and are passed off at such a rate that you do not possess as little as one cell of the body you had a year ago. You remember many years back, do you not? Many happenings or your childhood can be recalled to memory. How can you remember back through those many years when your brain is not yet a year old? Because you are mind. You are not body.

As an individual entity, functioning in an individual sphere, which is true of each one of us, you are all-powerful Mind and your body is the vehicle through which you function. You are master and your body is your servant. It is your instrument of expression. That is all.

Now, which is the real body – the one that remains pictured or imaged forever in mind as long as you exist here, or the one that decays in its entirety and passes into the earth every eleven months? And which are the real things – those things imaged or pictured in mind, or those things seen in the outer and which disintegrate after a short existence?

Right here I do not wish to have you misled into the impression that the outer is of little or no importance in human achievement, but it is only secondary, while a fundamental knowledge of the operation of mind is of primary importance to you at the start.

I wish it were possible to explain, so that you might understand, the process by which a picture in mind becomes objectified, but it would require hours to even make an effort in this direction, and then I might only confuse you. For words are feeble things when one attempts to explain these deeper things of Universal Law. One really must gradually and patiently advance up to and into them to understand. However, it is not necessary to know this in order to use the law any more than it is necessary to know the law by which the sun's rays are transmitted to earth in order to enjoy them. You have faith in my sincerity of purpose. Very well, place the same amount of faith in the power of this law and anything you undertake will be possible of accomplishment. Let us get on to the next step.

# Chapter Ten

You may have heard it said that there are many minds, but such a statement is merely an idiom. There is nothing in science or reality to support such a predicate. There is but one mind, as there is but one electricity, one air or atmosphere. The many minds referred to are but a multiplicity of expressions of the one. We use mind as we use air or electricity – as our individual needs require.

I will now ask that you bear with me for a time while I make use of a contradiction in order that I may simplify the next subject. It becomes necessary for me to refer to three minds, or, properly speaking, three phases of mind.

You are apparently made up of three minds. The one which controls the functioning of the body and which, for want of a better word, I will call the Deeper mind. This mind we are not particularly concerned with, and properly should not be. It knows its duties better than we do. We can cooperate with this mind to our great profit in both health and strength by keeping our thoughts off the body. By forgetting that we have a body and thereby refraining form interfering with the proper functioning of this Deeper mind, we will find that it will get along very nicely.

The other two minds in which we are greatly interested and with which we must deal from this time forth, are what I might name the Inner and Outer minds.

Those two minds you will readily recognize from the fact that when you take sides within yourself upon a subject and find yourself carrying on a spirited controversy with yourself, you are engaging these two minds.

The proper office of the Outer mind, which is in touch with external things through the medium of the five senses, is to transmit its desires to the Inner mind, which is the seat of power within you and which, by its very nature, has no consciousness of duality, since it has no faculty of discrimination. It knows no impossible, no failure, no obstacle, or limit or lack. It depends upon the guidance of the Outer mind and throws its great, unlimited force into anything that the Outer mind may direct.

I can better illustrate the character of the Inner mind by again comparing it with electricity. As electricity is the greatest power in the world, so is the Inner mind the greatest power in your being. Of themselves, neither operates independently, but depends upon a separate agency to incite them to action, and both bring helpful or harmful results according to the wisdom or ignorance with which they are directed.

This being true, how important, then, for the Outer to unite with the Inner and cooperate with it, and if this were the condition in human affairs, man would be master of his environment instead of being the slave of circumstance.

Why are all not super-men instead of merely men? For this reason: The Outer mind forms a desire which is automatically taken up by the Inner mind and, in turn, it immediately proceeds to function toward bringing it forth. It scarcely has time to turn its great force in that direction before the Outer has found a new fancy or has conjured up illusionary obstacles, and the Inner, not being on the surface, not in contact with outer things and consequently dependent upon the Outer for guidance, is forced to again divert its power. And thus it goes, on and on, like leaks in a steam pipe, scattering its wonderful power everywhere but getting nowhere.

Why is the Inner mind thus thwarted in every move it makes toward accomplishment? Why? Because the Outer judges everything by what the eye and ear reports and transmit that message to the Inner. What do we find humanity doing? We find them taking pictures of what they experience daily in the outer world, developing the sensitized film, then printing those pictures upon themselves within. The procedure should be just the reverse.

I know whereof I speak when I say that we have been endowed with the capacity and the power to create desirable pictures within and to find them automatically printed in the outer world of our environment. And it is a simple process, as you will see later. When we can do this, we have mastery. And not before.

Well, then, you would say, the need must be to discipline the Outer mind, since it seems to be the offender. Just so. But since it meets up with thousands of experiences almost daily, ordinary methods of training might require years to accomplish results. Or, at best, such training would be a long-drawn-out process. There is a quicker and better way. A method which, when put into operation, employs the usefulness of the Outer mind without taking into account its vacillating willfulness.

# Chapter Eleven

And the first step in this direction follows: We will suppose that there is an urgent need for you to reach a certain town as quickly as possible. When you step into your automobile, you naturally picture in mind a given point of destination and turn your face in that direction. If that point be distant, you may become diverted onto wrong roads many times, but upon noting this, you return and again take the proper course, guided by what? – by the picture in mind of the place you are headed for, and you get there.

You held to a set definite objective until you reached it. You held your objective or destination in mind without any particular effort or strain and merely returned the car to the proper road when you found that it had strayed, and you got there. Thus it is with us. A set definite objective must be established if we are to accomplish anything in a big way.

What do I mean by establishing a set definite objective? Is it as simple as it sounds? No, not at the start. Would you set your objective at a million immediately and start out thoughtlessly to make it overnight? Yes, you might, if you have the capacity to see a million as an immediate possibility. But this is quite rare. The wise thing to do is to grow to it as the marathon runner begins by first running a mile. Then he goes two miles, then three. Thus he expands his capacity to eventually cover the full distance.

Why is a set definite objective necessary? There are three reasons.

First – The Inner mind is the positive pole of your being, while the Outer is the negative pole, as in geology the North Pole is the positive and the South Pole the negative. There must be a positive and negative in everything in the universe in order to complete a circuit or circle, without which there would be no activity, no motion. To illustrate this, there would be no forward if we had no backward. There could be no up if there were no down. There never could have been such a quality as good if there were no evil, so called. How could there have been light without darkness? For us to be conscious of one thing, there must be another opposite by which to compare it or it remains nonexistent to us.

Now, in everything that is obedient to Law, the positive dominates and governs and the negative serves. But mankind reverses this. The Outer mind looks out upon the world and reports strife, competition, obstacles, impossibilities and similar conditions. Why? Because of the absence of direction, it is left to wander without a purpose and thus, aimlessly wandering, it accepts everything.

The set definite objective, firmly imaged or pictured in mind, immediately whips the Outer into line by giving it a fixed duty to perform. This, automatically, without any effort on your part, infuses into it the positive quality of the Inner mind, and since the law of the universe and, therefore, also of your being, cannot change; negative conditions, including individuals, serve it and therefore you. And again, automatically, positive conditions and individuals are attracted to you as surely as the steel particles are attracted to the magnet. That is the first reason.

Second – The atmosphere, or ether, as we prefer to name it, is filled with millions upon millions of thoughts which are forever in motion. The hundreds of stations in your country, all broadcasting simultaneously, give you a slight idea of the thoughts in the air. Every human being is a broadcasting station and everybody is a receiving set. This explains why I am able to answer your questions instantly, before you have had to form them into words. The fact that I have been getting your thoughts before you have expressed them and which have been puzzling you, is now made clear. This is a faculty developed after years of training. This faculty was always in me and is within you. I have brought out and made use of mine, while yours lies dormant almost entirely.

To get back to our subject. The man who has no set definite objective is tuning in to everything and getting nothing. He is unfortunate indeed, for he is at the mercy of millions of conflicting thoughts and his is a life of confusion and distress. Some of those in my work have so perfected themselves that they are able to see these thoughts by virtue of the same law developed in themselves, by which you will soon be enjoying motion pictures transmitted to you over the radio. Therefore, we know what we are talking about when we speak of the chaos of thoughts in the air.

On the other hand, the man who has a set definite objective deliberately tunes in to one thing, which action automatically makes him positive and consequently wipes out the others. If it is money he wants, he gets it. If it is position he wants, he gets it. Nothing that such a man tunes in to can be withheld from him.

Third – When you set your mind upon anything, whether it be small or large, a pencil, a hat, automobile, a home or great riches; whether it be tangible like these or intangible, such as an education, a profession or travel, you transfer a portion of your life force to that thing, or how could it be otherwise drawn to you? And you continue to nourish it as long as it is held in mind, and the intensity of your desire governs the power with which the force is directed.

So you can see that were even a positive man to direct his force at several objectives, that force becomes divided and each objective receives but a feeble stimulus, resulting in slow reaction or none at all. Have you a great ultimate goal to reach requiring the attainment of lesser objectives on the way? Well, then, let the many lie inactive and direct your force at the nearest or first, and that being accomplished, take up the next and thus follow on as they occur in sequential order.

Have I now given you the Law in its entirety? Well, in a sense, I have. Then again, I have not. To instruct one as to what to do is good, but to show one how to do it is better. It is not only necessary that we learn how to attain, but we must also learn how to maintain. I will, therefore, go further and give you an important requirement in successful achievement and that is secretiveness.

# Chapter Twelve

Before I explain the value of Secretiveness, I will have to change from our subject at hand for a while.

When you declare "I am," "I will," "I did," you are making a most mighty and profound utterance. There are very few who realize the power released when the "I" is expressed. Hear the great proclamation, "I AM THAT I AM," from the lips of the Prophet, which has lived and rung out down the ages and which, when understood, unites each one with that impersonal, universal power.

The body you have is personal, but the "I" you express is universal, for in all the universe there is but one "I," as in all the universe there is but one figure "1." The other figure "7," for instance, is the "1" repeated so many times. It is the understanding of those in my work that the "I" is the root from which the figure "1" has sprung.

From what I have said, you should be able to see this: That when you work in the "me" consciousness (Outer mind), you are working from the personal, limited standpoint. When you work in the "I" consciousness (Inner mind), you invoke and receive the help of the impersonal, unlimited resources of the universe. Well, you ask, How am I to arrive at this state? Easily, I will say. For by merely following the system of practice that I am outlining, you naturally gravitate into it unknowingly.

Now listen attentively: If there is but one "I" and you cannot express yourself without using it, it follows that as far as you individually are concerned, there must be but one "you." You do not get this clearly? Well, did you ever apply the pronoun "I" to any other human being? Of course you did not. You could not. You might say "he," "she," "they," "you," "we," but never "I." For there is but one "I" and that is you. And I say there is but one "you." Yes, applied individually, there is but one "you." We will suppose that through a slight accident, you were to be rendered unconscious for five minutes. During that period, the world would cease to exist. It would be absolutely wiped out. But, you will say, it would go on just the same. Yes, but without your consciousness of it, it is not; it is non-existent. Proving that there is but one You.

Since the great and mighty "I" is, when expressed individually, none other than yourself, you can see what power you have at your command. You can see what a wonderful being you are. You can see that you are now a master, not yet developed perhaps, but the qualities are there awaiting unfoldment and use.

If you do not clearly understand what I have just given, pass it by for this time and let us go on to the next. You can later reason it out for yourself and see the truth of it.

You might question the value of such detailed explanation, but I have a purpose and that purpose is to force you to think, to think deeply, with intensity. Right here I would not have you confuse the word intensity with tenseness. Tenseness implies mental strain and arises out of fear and anxiety. It is destructive to both mind and body. My use of intensity here suggests mental force or power and its results are constructive.

You know thus far that progress depends upon the degree of sustained intensity in a given direction. And you know that progress is very rapid these days. We must travel as rapidly as the world or give up, and when we give up we immediately begin to retrograde. To enjoy enduring success we should travel a little in advance of the world.

The persistent inner urge in the mind to reach an objective more speedily, eventually crystallized and out-pictured itself in the form of an automobile, which was the first big step in fast transportation for general use. But since if it is the nature of Mind to forever reach out for greater achievement, the airplane came into being in obedience to the mind of man to find a way faster and not subject to the obstacles incident to automobile travel. And thus Mind moves and thus it will move forever.

Open your eyes and look about you. Cannot you discern the trend? Mind is forever reaching out and has not stopped at the airplane as a rapid mode of travel. I hesitate to tell you what the next great step in this direction will be, but I will tell you this: Mind is so rapidly coming into its own, that in the not too distant future, the man who knows the law and uses it will be supreme and the ignorant one who refuses to see this will just remain in bondage to his false beliefs. How important, then, to learn the law of thinking things through rather than follow the time-worn method of attempting to force them through. One is mastery and the other slavery.

Returning to the subject, the value of secretiveness lies in the fact that, being impersonal and universal, the "I" throws its power in with whatever words it is coupled, and when your plans are expressed in words verbally, they become realized and their force is spent. The Outer mind has found a way of escape and your purpose has lost its necessary momentum.

# Chapter Thirteen

The next requisite I might term your Nourishment or Reserve. We know that few are capable of sustained effort, and that is the reason why we have comparatively few outstanding successes. You have learned that your great power lies not upon the surface but deep within your being, in your Inner mind. The average human lives upon the surface, ignorant of his great interior power. Placing what little faith he has, in the Outer mind, he is governed by its false reports, and as a result he is constantly in a turmoil of confusion, strife and strain until he succumbs, discouraged and disheartened, broken in health and spirit.

Why is this so? Why is it a common expression that a man who accumulates wealth pays dearly for it in health and vitality? Because, as I have already told you, when he intensifies upon a given objective, he automatically transfers to it a portion of his vital life force. This is all very well and necessary, but such a practice continued, with no replenishment to keep that life force nourished, drains it and the result is trouble.

It is your rightful heritage, your birthright, to have anything that you desire and without limit, for, as I have said, you are in a sense the only one here, for yours is the only consciousness in existence as far as you are concerned. You can never know another. Those things that you desire were put here for you to use and enjoy. If not, why are they here? And since only you can be conscious of your own individual desires, those things were placed here specifically for you.

Yes, you may have riches and position and with them health and happiness, when you know the law of your being and cooperate with it. I have no patience with the one who proclaims that poverty is a blessing. Poverty is the greatest curse upon earth. The one who preaches such a doctrine is untrue to himself, for, while such remarks are proceeding from his lips, the desire for the good things of life is gnawing at his heart.

Knowing so well that each individual, being differently constituted, given the fundamental principles of the Law, will each work it out somewhat differently, accordingly to his own particular inherent nature, I have purposely avoided referring to my method, so that you might have your entire freedom of interpretation and decision. But since I feel prompted to do so, I will give you a hint of how I work, advising that you let this not influence or change you in your method, because of it having come from me. You cannot attain dominion patterning after another, or following custom or tradition. Sheep and plodders do that. Masters and leaders never do.

A painting would be a dull, uninteresting thing were the artist, in featuring a great oak tree, to fail to include its natural surroundings of grass, brush, flowers, leaves, and possibly sky and clouds. The true artist creates a faithful reproduction. Our methods are similar. While he places his upon the canvas, I place mine within. He places the oak upon the canvas and gives it its natural surroundings. I do the same. To bring his picture forth, he is compelled to concentrate upon it to the exclusion of all else that would tend to draw him away from his purpose. So am I. At times something in the external suggests the picture to him. At other times, inspiration suggests it. It is the same with me. A hundred things in a day may come up to distract him and attempt to draw him away, but with his picture uppermost, he does not resist those distractions, but gives them their due attention and returns to the picture. Just so with me. His picture completed, he begins another. I also do. For I am never consciously, mentally inactive. Inactivity is retrogression.

Should I desire the presence of my servant at this moment, I would see him before me in my mind picture surrounded by what is within my vision here and shortly the picture out-pictures.

Were I to desire wealth, I would surround that picture with all of wealth's natural accompaniments of conditions and possessions that would instinctively present themselves for inclusion. I would get my suggestions, if necessary, from the out-picturing or externalized picture of another's success. I would go about my duties as usual. It matters little what I appear to be doing in the outer. It matters much what I am doing within.

If I were a beginner and desired, for instance, a new automobile or home, I would select a picture in colors of the one or closely resembling the one I desired, from a trade or home periodical, and place it where it would meet my eyes frequently. This would tend to hold the Outer mind in line and hasten the out-picturing of my idea.

# Chapter Fourteen

I will now give you a list of powerful words which will not only tend to keep the life force nourished, but also to bear you up, sustain and carry you through whenever the strength each particular word creates, is needed:

CONCENTRATION

PEACE

POISE

HARMONY

GOOD-WILL

NON-RESISTANCE

JUSTICE

FREEDOM

**John McDonald**

GUIDANCE

WISDOM

UNDERSTANDING

Return to top

INSPIRATION

INTELLIGENCE

MEMORY

LAW AND ORDER

FAITH

CONFIDENCE

SPIRIT

HEALTH

STRENGTH

ENERGY

ACTIVITY

VITALITY

POWER

58

LIFE

YOUTH

SUCCESS

HAPPINESS

ALERTNESS

RESOURCEFULNESS

PERSISTENCE

PURPOSE

ACHIEVEMENT

MASTERY

DOMINION

After the day's activities devoted to your ordinary duties and affairs and the consequent devitalization of your life force, more or less, it is well to set apart an hour or half hour, as your judgment might dictate, each evening when you can be alone and undisturbed, and in the quiet and stillness of your own being, take each word separately down the list, or if you feel so disposed, select such words from the list as you feel your particular needs require at the time. Firmly impress your being with each word and at the same time, interpreting its meaning and its effect upon you, not necessarily in the terms of its generally accepted meaning, but strictly as it appeals to you.

Although I am continuing to impress you with the fact that you are the "I," the power in your world, and that you are to stand upon your own two feet firmly and live it – not particularly display it, but live it – (great characters shrink from display and publicity because of the littleness of it) yet I do not advise that the declaration "I am" be used in connection with these words unless you are at the time in a positive frame of mind; unless you have a full conviction of what you are repeating.

To declare, for example, "I am Power," lays the Inner mind open to attack from the Outer in the form of denial or doubt. Whereas, when the words are only repeated, they do not take upon themselves the nature of declaration, and consequently the Outer mind has not been given the opportunity to become aroused in opposition.

To simplify explanation of your right attitude during this practice, I might say that keeping your thoughts off the body and off external affairs and things, automatically places you in the ideal mood. Of course, the Outer mind will wander and bring up hundreds of things, hundreds of times, but like the automobile that I mentioned becoming diverted on to the wrong road, you bring it back and bring it back, each time setting it on the right road. This wandering propensity of the Outer mind will gradually lessen during these periods and you will find yourself becoming a master of concentration.

There should be no strain, striving, anxiety or concern connected with this practice. You devote each evening, unless otherwise taken up by occasional business, social or family duties, to allowing these words to sink in and penetrate your being and like drops of pure water entering a vessel of impure water, drop by drop the non-essentials are forced out and the essentials remain.

These powerful words, acting upon you (your being) in the same way that food does upon your body, automatically find their own needed places and uses within, in the same manner as do the elements in the food which you eat, and you should not look for results from this practice any more than you look for results from what you eat daily. You are to practice this system every evening as regularly and diligently as your affairs will permit and then forget them entirely until the next evening. They will be doing their work below the surface unknown to you, but their effects will show forth in you and your affairs.

**John McDonald**

# Chapter Fifteen

Approaching the close of your instructions, I believe it well to outline an example of procedure for you. Since, as I have previously said, words are often so inadequate to convey the proper meaning when dealing with a subject of this kind, I will approach facts from different angles for better elucidation.

Here is an example: Invoking the aid of this law, neither money, friends or influence are necessary to the attainment of whatever your heart is set upon.

Whether you are a banker, a clerk or a bootblack, it is no respecter of person or position. Whether your ambition lies in direct line with the position you are now occupying, or whether it necessitates an entire change from what you are doing. You may have no definite plan in life except the fact that you want to get ahead. Since all the desire in the world will get you nowhere, it becomes necessary that a definite objective be first arrived at and then firmly established within.

After intelligent deliberation you decide upon one Supreme Goal. It is distant, perhaps, but the glorious assurance is that it can be attained. What is your first step? If a banker or merchant, is it a definite increase in volume monthly? Or, if an employee, is it a position above? There, you have your first and nearest objective in the direction of your Supreme Objective.

When the first objective is reached, what then? Set another one beyond that, immediately. Why? Because the perculiar nature of the Outer mind is to drop back into inertia after being forced through to an objective. You can imagine the Outer mind reflecting something after this fashion: "Well, I have been mercilessly whipped about and forced through to that thing, but I reached it and now I will have a rest." And your answer will be: "No rest for you, for I have already started you upon another." Because, once having attained that valuable momentum, maintain it. Cling to it. And as the momentum increases, the steps in your progress become more rapid, until eventually it will be possible to reach an objective almost immediately, as is the practice of those in my work.

The course followed in bringing forth your objective can be likened exactly to the process that takes place in a seed. Being fixed in the darkness of the soil, it proceeds to express or out-picture the exact picture held within its life cell and, in obedience to law, it sends up a shoot seeking the light. At the same time, it sends down roots seeking nourishment. If, on the way up, that shoot encounters obstacles in any form, it does not attempt to force them out of its way. It travels around them. If the roots fail to find the required nourishment, it withers away. If all goes well, it blossoms forth and, having reached its goal, a seed is again dropped and the process repeated. Bear in mind that the actual process takes place in darkness, beneath the surface. Thus it is with us. That is where all great and important ideas are developed.

Now, are you going to cast glances out of the corner of your eye to see how the thing is proceeding? Are you going to set to wondering how the thing works, or if it really is working? Not at all. You set the objective. You therefore planted the seed. You would not dig up a seed in your garden to see if it were sprouting. You planted and watered it and are satisfied that, according to the law of its being, it will come forth. Likewise, nothing upon earth can prevent your objective from becoming externalized, because nothing in the world can nullify Universal Law. You plant the seed idea. You hold it there. You nourish it. You have done your part. Trust the Law to do its part.

Will you encounter resistance? Oh, yes. Your activity creates it. Why? Because action requires reaction to support it. Resistance is the negative pole of action or activity, the positive pole as you have already heard, and you need both. If there were no resistance, action would be nonexistent.

It is resistance that keeps the airplane soaring. Without resistance, it could not fly. Neither could the birds; or the fish swim; or you walk. As the power of the engine increases, the greater the momentum of the airplane and the greater the resistance necessary to support it. The greater the momentum, the greater the altitude or height possible to attain. With the decrease in engine power comes the decrease in momentum and the consequent dropping of the plane.

This is an example for us. Momentum must be attained and then maintained if we are to reach the heights of achievement. And the work is delightful after the apparent difficulty of the first steps are passed. For there is nothing more joyous than the satisfaction of having achieved something worth while.

Are you to recognize resistance in any guise? No. For, if you recognize it as a power opposed to your progress, you are resisting it, therefore you automatically acknowledge it as a power greater than you, for no lesser power can retard the progress of a greater one. That is plain. And going further, remember this great truth: Whoever or whatever you resist, be it in thought, word or action; be it in the form of criticism, envy, jealousy, hatred or otherwise, you must assuredly help, and you weaken yourself proportionately. Why? Because you have deliberately taken a portion of your precious life force so necessary to your progress, and transferred it to that person or thing. Have you not witnessed the case at times, of one becoming exhausted after a "fit of rage" over another? Exhaustion is depletion. And to deplete means to empty. Something went out. Yes, to the other person to his profit and the other's loss. This is an example of the transfer of life force in a violent form. You are very fortunate in having learned this wisdom. Now, by all means, practice it.